Ouida Manus
to
Delores Sobowale
Thanks so much!

LONGING FOR ETERNITY

DERRICK MARCUS

Copyright © 2020 Derrick Marcus

All rights reserved. No part of this book may be reproduced or used in any manner without written permission of the copyright owner except for the use of quotations in a book review.

ISBN: 9781074846848

This book is dedicated to my brother

Donald "Mugga" Garcia

R.I.P

TABLE OF CONTENTS

Preface   1

Chapter 1: My Past

A Baby is Born   5

Ghetto Kids, Ghetto Life   6

My Family   7

My Destiny   8

My Family (part 2)   9

The Horrors Under the Moon   10

Of Boys and Men   12

Grip My Sword   13

Chasin' This Money   14

My Ambitions   16

Young Hustlas   18

Real Life   20

One Man Army   21

Untitled   22

Concrete Jungle   23

'Cause I Don't Have Love   25

Monster   27

Losing a Friend   28

Smokin' Until…   29

Lost in My Thoughts   30

Your First Enlightenment   32

Leave Me Be   33

F*** Everything   35

Chapter 2: My Present

Love Ain't Hard to Find   41

Longing for Eternity   43

Running to the Future   44

Just a Nigga   45

Praying for Healing   47

So Intoxicated   48

Save Me from Myself   50

My Closest Roaddogz   52

Ice Cream in the Rain   53

Stressed   55

Again   56

If It's a Boy   57

Letting Go of the Past   59

Remember   60

The Great Potter   62

A Stronger Love   63

The Good Life   64

Untitled 2   66

Trying to Change   67

My Spirit Drops   69

Anger, Anxiety, Ambitions   71

Chapter 3: My Future

A New Life   75

My Contribution   76

Oh, What a Dream   77

Jackpot   78

The Devil Tryna Stop Me   79

Love to Live to Learn   81

Ghetto Profit   82

R.E.B.E.L. L.I.F.E   83

Bumpy Roads   84

Thank You God   85

Until It's Over   87

When My Time Comes   88

Letter to My Child   89

Finally, Eternity   91

PREFACE

I believe that God gives everyone their spirit. Given from God, our spirit inside has a greatness far beyond our physical being. Our spiritual being – the true us – can be sought after by becoming closer to God. Yet our physical being goes through worldly experiences that keep us from doing so. For example, we fall victim to emotions, temptations, and everyday situations in life that keep us disconnected from God. Only when we are free from these distractions of life and the world around us can we get closer to God and experience our spiritual being and its potential. The first part of the battle is actually realizing the things that stray us away from God. The second part is the struggle to change by resisting those things. Eternity is the name that I have given to my own spiritual being. My longing for Eternity is my wish to someday experience my true spiritual potential as I struggle through the trials and tribulations of life and battle with myself to change.

MY PAST

A Baby is Born

A baby is born

Blind to the ways of the world

But soon he must learn

Ghetto Kids, Ghetto Life

Dedicated to my sister, Nae-nae

Gettin' up out the bed yawnin'
Scrambled eggs and white rice in the mournin'
Sliced spiced ham or turkey
Drinkin' Kool-Aid when we're thirsty
Mm, mm, now that's good
Now that's breakfast in the hood
We ghetto to our core
Stealin' candy from the store
I'ma sell some at school to make some money
We wasn't blessed with milk and honey
Momma braidin' our hair 'cause it's frizzy
Our imaginations are keepin' us busy
Bangin' on the floor, singin' and rappin'
Sometimes we cryin', sometimes we laughin'
Ain't got much but we got each other
Two ghetto kids, sister and brother

My Family

My family, my family

Can't live with them, can't live without them

Theres so many things that I can say about them

Some good, some bad, but I will say

Until I die, all I'll ever need

Is my family, my family indeed

My Destiny

Sometimes I leave the present behind
I travel through time in my mind
In my mind's eye I see my fate
A great future that awaits
I marvel at the thought of the future me
An astonishing man yet to be
I get a feeling of ecstasy
Just thinking about my destiny

My Family (part 2)

My family, my family

We're broken apart

My mother and father on separate sides

Of my now broken heart

Things shattered between them

Leaving love lost in the dust

My family, My family

What happened to us?

The Horrors Under the Moon

As the day slips into the night

And the gleaming sun starts to fall

Horrors occur under the moon

And a young boy bears witness to them all

He's supposed to be getting sleep

And resting for school the next day

But instead he is forced into the streets

Where the thugs and drug addicts come out to play

He is led by his own father

In and out of multiple drug spots

And while he follows along

His virgin eyes are experiencing a lot

Have you ever witnessed people crave for drugs

As if they are about to die?

Have you ever watched somebody

Commit sexual acts just to get high?

Imagine being eleven years old
Watching people smoke crack all night
And with so much going on around you
You even have to be prepared to fight

The sun will rise again in about a hour
It will be time to go to school soon
A young boy will be left with memories
Of the horrors that occur under the moon

Of Boys and Men

I am young but I stand tall

Amongst the men

I watch how they hustle

And I proceed to hustle just like them

I absorb their wisdom

And I grow smarter

I feed off of their energy

And I go harder

I am surrounded by guys

Who are twice my size

But I walk with my head to the sky

And ambition in my eyes

You're either a boy or a man

In this world we live in

I am a boy who has been forced

To be a man amongst the men

Grip My Sword

I am forced to be a soldier

Constantly preparing for war

A war I instantly become part of

Once I leave my front door

Where I'm from, not every day is blessed

With peace and tranquility

Most of the time I am surrounded

By violence and hostility

The only way I can survive

Is by gripping my sword

And going to jail is something

That I can't afford

But even if I have to spend life

In the pen

At least I'll live another day

To grip my sword again

Chasin' This Money

Better days are on the way
I know, 'cause I had a taste of them
After I chased some money

These dollars I got now will be spent soon
So I will be replacing them
Gotta chase more money

Ain't nothing better to do
Than what I'm doing now
And that's chasin money

If you're wondering what you can do
To better your problems, I know how
Go chase some money

Things I used to do for fun are relics of the past
Now what I do to have a blast

Is chase money

Some people chase dreams, some chase love
Now ain't that funny?
I'm just gonna keep chasin' this money

My Ambitions

My ambitions

Running through me like wild horses

Stampeding at top speed,

Giving me the adrenaline I need

To do what I have to do to succeed.

My ambitions

Like a boxer with a heavyweight hit,

Knocking out every reason

That there is to quit.

My ambitions

When I hear "you can't" from any man,

My ambitions are the ones who convince me I can.

My ambitions

They have helped me to get through the most

Complexed obstacles

My ambitions give me the confidence to attempt
What seems like the impossible.

My ambitions
Help me cook up victories that taste so delicious,
I can never lose faith
I can only be ambitious.

Young Hustlas

OG Hustla: What's goin' on lil homie

Young Hustla: Yo wattup OG

OG Hustla: I see you out here hustlin'

Young Hustla: Yeah you know how it be

OG Hustla: Whatchu doin' on these streets?

Young Hustla: My brothers and sisters gotta eat

OG Hustla: Where ya parents at?

Young Hustla: I don't live with moms, and pops be smokin' crack

OG Hustla: Well holla if you need me lil bro

Young Hustla: For sure OG, good lookin' out yo

Real Life

So this is what life really is?

Sometimes I wish that I was still a kid

Before I realized how hard it is to survive

When it was actually more fun being alive

I dreamt of the day that I'd be a young man

Didn't know I'd have to live with weapons in hand

I was blind to the evils that roamed these streets

The devil was a stranger to me, but now we meet

I thought that love would always be a friend to me

Turns out we're actually becoming enemies

I'm not saying that happiness was always mine

But the older I get its been harder to find

I get intoxicated and drift off into a fools paradise

How else can I keep my sanity?

This is the reality of life

One Man Army

I am a one man army

In this war that life has declared

Always ready to indulge in battle

I am not scared, I am prepared

Adjusting to being a loner

As I get older

Picture one man

With the heart of a thousand soldiers

I will conquer every battle of this war

On my own

In the end I will celebrate in victory

Alone

Untitled

Always running to the future

In too much of a hurry to

Stop long enough to taste the fruit

The beauty of the tree catches

My eyes as I pass by

As always

I pause

For a second or two

To enjoy its sight

Its grand trunk and

Pretty leaves

Oh, and I bet the fruit is so sweet

And again I tell myself

I'll try one the next time I pass by

Concrete Jungle

In a wilderness that never sleeps, a young man

Treks the five boroughs of the jungle

He is no stranger to the night sky

They have known each other since

He was a boy

The moon

The stars

They follow him

Keeping him company as he roams

Alone

Some of the beasts of the wild

Takes a liking to him

They are older

So he soaks up their' wisdom

Inheriting their' knowledge of surviving

The evils of the jungle

He is ambitious

He strives

Not just to survive

But to prevail

'Cause I Don't Have Love

Girls come and go for me

The way the night comes and the day leaves

I spend only one night with them

Sometimes more than one night if I please

If one holds my attention for too long

Eventually I disown her

I'm not a bad guy

I'm just addicted to being a loner

'Cause I don't have love

My heart wants to love

But my brain won't let it

My heart did love once

But my brain told my heart to forget it

I don't have love with any of them

But I have fun with them all

When I get tired of one girl

I just give the next one a call

'Cause I don't have love

Monster

I got plans to do big things

Be successful and live a great life

When I close my eyes

I see myself becoming an extraordinary man

But when my eyes are open

And I am viewing the world around me

All I can see is me turning into

A monster

This is a crazy, vicious and scary world

I do not want to be a monster

But how else can I survive?

Losing a Friend
Dedicated to my bestie, Joanna

A friendship so great

Too bad we let it crumble

Will the sorrow cease?

Smokin' Until...

I'll be smokin' until everything that has yet to be
has happened
and everything that currently exists
has faded into a memory.
Until then, I'll be smokin'.
And I won't stop smokin' until Nature
has grown tired of the conventional laws
that she governs us by;
when she allows us to grow Mary Jane,
not by planting seeds in dirt,
but with the power of our minds.
Until that happens,
I'll be smokin'.
Smokin' until my afterlife begins
or until this blunt ends.
But then I'll just roll another one up
and smoke again.

Lost in My Thoughts

Lost in my thoughts

Friends with my own mind

Talking to myself inside my head

Because I hate talking to people sometimes

Lost

Somewhere between Ambition Street and Anger Avenue

Right around the corner from hate

Trying to get to Happiness Boulevard before it's too late

But I'm lost

Trying to find the center of my soul

Escaping the present is my goal

When I am overwhelmed by the world

And yearning to be alone

I close my eyes and enter a world of my own

This world is home

This world is mine

And I am lost in the thoughts

Of a futuristic state of mind

Most people will choose to be surrounded

By something familiar at any cost

Me, I'd rather be by myself

And lost

Your First Enlightenment

There comes a time we all experience

At some point in our lives

When we are met by a truth of reality

That opens up our closed eyes

What we were blinded to before

And didn't have the power to see

Becomes very clear to us

We now see it so easily

This knowledge we suddenly stumble upon

Comes to us so unexpected

But now that we obtain it

It would be a shame for it to be neglected

This experience we undergo

Makes us no longer think the same

So begins a brand new life

When enlightenment sparks our brain

Leave Me Be

Leave me be

In my four corner room

Loneliness and me

Like a bride and her groom

Leave me be

And don't bother me

While I continue reciting lyrics

To keep my sanity

Leave me be

The time that I spend

Is by myself, composing music

Not having fun with friends

If you were like me

If you could see what I see

You would stay to yourself too

So leave me be

F*** Everything

Family used to be my top priority

Until I started seeing through lies

The love they seem to show

Is not corresponding with the look in their' eyes

Loyalty is starting to look like betrayal in disguise

So now I'm thinking

F*** family

I tried to build friendships

To understand why people cherish them so

The reasons why

I probably will never know

Because all I've seen is friendships come and go

So now I'm thinking

F*** friends

Being moral is something

That I wish to be

But how can I do good

When only bad is done to me

Fighting fire with fire is the only means

Of survival that I see

So now I'm thinking

F*** morality

I yearn for love like everybody else

But it is hard to find

I'm starting to think that it exists

Only in the mind

I want to love but love is blind

So now I'm thinking

F*** love

I used to care about things a lot

Those caring feelings

Are starting to rot

Everything that I thought life was

It really is not

So now I'm thinking

F*** everything

MY PRESENT

Love Ain't Hard to Find

Dedicated to my wife, Shaniqua

I found love on Merrick Boulevard

I never saw her before

So I had no clue who she was

When I spotted her standing in front of the store

Honestly when I think about it

Its actually kind of funny

Because I wasn't looking for love

I was really looking for money

I didn't bother to look for love

Because money was treating me so good

I doubted that love could make me feel

The way that money could

On my determined search for money

Love stopped me in my tracks

I walked pass her, but a magnetic force

Pulled me to turn back

I turned back towards her

I couldn't resist

Even in this moment

I believed that love didn't exist

Her eye contact sparked a feeling

That I never experienced before

Unfamiliar with love, I was blind

To what was standing in front of that store

After getting to know her better

I realized who she was

I then knew that

I had finally found love

So to those who search for love

Here's a word to you all

Sometimes love ain't hard to find

When you ain't looking for it at all

Longing for Eternity

I am longing to see

The greatness of Eternity

But this present moment is feeling like a forever

I guess I'll just

Kill time and pass it by

Pass it by as I fly

Fly right pass the forevers and

Wave at them goodbye

And before I know it

I shall see

The greatness of Eternity

Running to the Future

Running to the future
Running from the past
Running right pass the present
But getting nowhere fast

Just a Nigga

I have the potential

To achieve something great

To be legendary

It is my fate

But to them, I'm just a nigga

I am a product

Of adversity and ambition

I am the caterpillar

After it transitions

But to them, I'm just a nigga

I am not

What they expect of me

I am a black rebel

Resisting conformity

But to them, I'm just a nigga

I am a king

I am a man

I am a god

But I understand

That to them, I'm just a nigga

Praying for Healing

I cry as I pour water into the dirt

Because I have damaged my health and it hurts

Seeing my pedals crumble up

And my roots so dry

I took advantage of the little things

Like sunlight from the sky

I now regret what I did wrong

As I look at my stem that once stood so strong

I am a beautiful plant

But my green leaves are turning brown and peeling

I lie dormant in the garden

Praying to God for my healing

So Intoxicated

When my problems get too tough

And life starts to get too rough

I just wanna get so intoxicated

And when I feel I can't take no more

And I'm ready to straight go off

I just wanna get so intoxicated

I get so, so intoxicated

When my temper is hot

Lately, I've been getting intoxicated a lot

When my thoughts are racing too fast

And I start dwelling on the past

It makes me wanna get so intoxicated

I get so, so intoxicated

I get so, so high

To keep me from feeling like I wanna cry

When anxiety sits in me

Or my anger gets to me

I just wanna get so intoxicated

I get so, so intoxicated

All the drugs and liquor

Just allows me to get angry quicker

Sometimes if I get too intoxicated

I don't know how to act

I love getting intoxicated

It don't love me back

But I still get so intoxicated

Save Me from Myself

Dear father God please

I need your help

I need you to save me

Save me from myself

I have not the time to worry

About my other adversaries

Because I seem to be

My biggest enemy

Putting myself in situations

That are full of complications

And constantly hurting myself

By damaging my health

Why do I do this?

I do not know

Why do I constantly continue

To be my own foe?

Dear father God please
I'm begging you for help
Please won't you save me
Save me from myself

My Closest Roaddogz

Dedicated to my brother, Mike

Under the sun we run the streets together

Chasin' after dollars

When the moon sits in the sky

We recollect our hustlin' hours

Chillin' outside, having conversations

About money-makin' operations

I take a drink

And I think

This is the life of me

And my closest roaddogz

Ice Cream in the Rain

Dedicated to my wife, Shaniqua

Do you notice how happy kids get
On a nice, sunny day when
The ice cream truck comes
Driving by?

Do you also notice the destitute of happiness,
When a cloudy, rainy day
Keeps the kids from coming
Out to play?

Lately, these days together have been
Feeling like those cloudy, rainy days.
The thunder is roaring extremely loud.
The lightning is flashing.

The rain is starting to come down very hard.
Dark clouds are hovering over

Our relationship.

But when we make love, it's like having

Ice cream in the rain.

Stressed

My heart is getting cold

My head is getting hot

My body is sitting still

But my mind is not

In a dark room

I am being held up by a chair

Staring into the air

With my mind's eye, I see my anger, my anxiety

And my ambitions engage in warfare

Negative thoughts spread throughout my mind

Like a disease

My optimism crumbles up and fall

Like dry leaves on autumn trees

And to my enemies

If you choose to disturb such a man

Then prepare yourself

For the wrath of my stress

Again

Last night was a great spectacle

That the upcoming night will transcend

We sang, danced, and laughed in intoxication

And this evening we'll do it again

Religious people might say we're wrong

They'd say we're committing sin

Drugs and alcohol induced conversation

Sexual actions of women and men

We splurge like it's our last day

We never miss the money we spend

We only live in the moment we're in

Until the night has come to an end

The rising sun is our alarm clock

A new day shall begin

Today we live for the future

And tonight we'll live for the moment

Again

If It's a Boy

If it's a girl

She'll probably give me hell

Make me scream and yell

But maybe I'll learn how to properly

Love a female

If it's a girl

I'd make her feel pretty

But I'd also make her tough

So she could know how to survive

When life gets rough

If it's a girl

I'll probably be overprotective

Interrogate her like a detective

She wouldn't understand my perspective

If it's a girl

She'll be daddy's little girl

The greatest daughter in the whole wide world

But if it's a boy

I just pray that he'll be

An even greater man than me

Letting Go of the Past

I'm depressed over the idea

That my past has a hold on me

When really I'm holding on

To my past

So much into my feelings that

I just won't let go of it

So busy caught up in the past

I am walking pass present opportunities

Never getting to my future blessings

So busy dwelling on the rain that

Poured in the year 2000

My eyes fail to notice the sun that

Shines in 2016

So busy reflecting on the battles I've loss

Not realizing that once I

Let go of the past

I will have won the war

Remember

Dedicated to Grandpa James (RIP)

You taught me many things

Throughout our times together

Many things that I

Still hold on too

I remember going through

Some very stormy weather

And being comforted by

Words of wisdom from you

I remember times

When I was blind

And you gave me the knowledge

That helped me see

Now that you're gone

Inside of my mind

I remember the lessons

you taught to me

On my journey as a man

You made me better

Guiding me through

The things men go through

As time goes on

I'll always remember

The words of wisdom

That were given by you

The Great Potter

Dedicated to my daughter, Janelle

A work of art is what God has made of me

A masterpiece for all of the world to see

I stood before him like a piece of clay

And he worked on me day after day

The greatest potter he must be

To create all people great, even me

Now he has made me a potter too

And my piece of clay is you

My child, I shall mold you with all of my heart

Into a great work of art

A Stronger Love

Dedicated to my mother, Melissa

…and then we were happy

As if we never parted

You called to me, "Junior"

And I called to you, "Momma"

And my love for you was

Stronger than it ever was

The Good Life

We lay back in laughter

I play in your hair

She is crawling around everywhere

Smiling back at us in cheer

We bond as a family

With love in the air

From my eye falls joy

In the form of a tear

I was blind but now

To the future I stare

Before I couldn't

But now I hear

I listen as happiness

Whisper in my ear

We are delighted at the sight

Of our child we have here

Suddenly I lose focus

Of any worry or care

And I realize

How good life feels

Untitled 2

Paying the tree no attention

I walked pass it day after day

Until one sunny day

My eyes were blinded by sun rays

And my skin was

Overwhelmed by the heat that the sun made

The tree came to my aid

Providing me with shade

I loved her for that

Every now and then I still

Sit in her shade

Trying to Change

I'm trying to change
My habitual ways
What some might call of sin

I'm trying to change
And fight the temptations
That I hold within

I'm trying to change
And leave the evil thoughts
I have behind

I'm trying to change
The anger I have
Into positivity in my mind

I really want to
Change the world

But I can't change anyone else

Because I'm having
So much difficulty
Trying to change myself

I want to change
My life around
And live peacefully

But if I change
How will I survive
The evils around me?

My Spirit Drops

Dedicated to my brother, Mugga (RIP)

I listen through the phone

They tell me what happened

My mind locks

The world stops

My spirit drops

Thoughts and feelings

Spring up inside me

The questions grow

I want to know

Why you had to go

I have to tell our little sister Nae-nae

That you are gone

Tears hit the floor

The sorrow she endures

Down to her core

I try to go on

Without falling apart

With all the pain

I continue to sustain

I struggle to be sane

As life goes on

Sometimes I think of you

And my mind locks

The world stops

My spirit drops

Anger, Anxiety, Ambitions

Anger

I should care but I don't

I need to calm down but I wont

Why did my brother have to die?

I have a fire burning in my eyes

I want the world to pay for my pain

I feel like I'm going insane

I am eager to release this anger

Even if I put myself in danger

Anxiety

My mind is full of worries

They are making my vision blurry

I am focused on what-ifs

I feel my faith starting to drift

Will I survive these negative forces?

My negative thoughts are racing horses

My optimistic thoughts disappear

I can't find peace of mind anywhere

Ambitions

My anger and anxiety continue to stress me

But I won't let it get the best of me

I've succeeded through adversity before

And I will succeed once more

Despite my current situation

I will conquer all tribulations

I won't let anger stop my grind

I won't let anxiety control my mind

MY FUTURE

A New Life

Does God have a new life in store for me?
I wanna finally be able to escape poverty
I wanna finally be able to escape the pain
I know there's sunshine after the rain
I wanna be able to live without stressing
I'm ready to receive my awaited blessings
A new life with new goals and accomplishments
Achievements that will cause astonishment
After all the drama and disruption I need tranquility
I need peace and positivity for my family
I know that to receive change I must change too
I am ready to do what I have to do
I am ready to let the past be the past
And begin my new life at last

My Contribution

My contribution to the world

It will be of intense effort

That will positively impact people

The words that I speak

They will be an extension of my wisdom

That will enlighten someone

My actions

They will manifest positive outcomes

That someone will profit from

My accomplishments

They will be the results of hard work

That will motivate someone

The books that I write

They will be mentally stimulating

And they will inspire someone

My children

They will inherit my wisdom

And they will do the same

Oh, What a Dream

Dedicated to Jaylen, my unborn child

I dream of the day that

I'll get to see your face

My thoughts race

At a fast pace

As I imagine you being a reality

I envision your personality

I look at your mother and I visualize

The combination of us two

Into one beautiful you

The greatest thing

That my world has never seen

Oh, what a dream

Jackpot

My #1 goal used to be wealth

Now I'm hustlin' for health

Getting rich in healing

Is the greatest feeling

My brain used to be broke

It ain't no joke

Now I got wisdom to share

And knowledge to spare

I learned that spiritual needs

Are more important than materialistic greed

So I seeked God

And I hit the jackpot

The Devil Tryna Stop Me

My life has been turning

Completely around

I feel myself rising

Before I was down

But the devil doesn't like

To see me winning

He wants to control me

Like he did in the beginning

I feel like God and the devil

Are playing tug-a-war with me

The devil is pulling hard

So that God won't have all of me

Anytime my life is going

In the right direction

He stands in my way

With great objection

He baits me with negativity

Hoping that I fail

I'm only human so sometimes I might slip up

But I won't let him prevail

He got the best of me

A couple of times before

The devil always tryna stop me

But he won't stop me no more

Love to Live to Learn

There was a time
When my thoughts were irate
When my heart was full of hate
Then I learned to love

God gave me a reason to
Hold my head up high
I told pessimism goodbye
And I began loving to live

The wisdom I gained
Is now my eyes
To see life's ultimate prize
So now I live to learn

Ghetto Profit

Dedicated to 2Pac and Nipsey Hussel

I have introduced to them the means

Of living a life of freedom.

Will they now follow me,

The way the night follows the day,

As I lead them into a

World of liberty?

Or will they choose to remain trapped,

Only appreciating me after

I am gone?

R.E.B.E.L. L.I.F.E.

R – Resist the urge to conform

E – Excel beyond the norm

B – Being defiant towards indoctrination

E – Exceed expectations

L – Learning is liberation

L – Leaving conventional beliefs behind

I – Introducing enlightenment to your mind

F – Facing judgement and critique

E – Empowered by being unique

Bumpy Roads

Life isn't a smooth ride

That I know

I've been on some bumpy roads before

And now me and adversity

Meet again

Like old friends reunited

With a love-hate relationship

After all, how could I despise adversity

Its merciless challenges made me the man

I am today

I survived bumpy roads before

And I will again

Thank You God

Thank you, God, for providing me

The strength to withstand

The trials and tribulations

That are condemned to man

Thank you for the life

That you gave me to live

Thank you for the love

That you always give

Thank you for the times

You made me feel strong

When I was stressing

And struggling to carry on

I know that those hard times

Were not for naught

And I thank you for the lessons

And the knowledge that they brought

I thank you for the good

As well as the bad

I thank you for the family
And the friends that I had
Thank you for making me
Feel like I'm worth it
Thank you for your mercy
When I didn't deserve it
Thank you for giving me
A positive attitude
I thank you because you are
Deserving of my gratitude

Until It's Over

I've been going strong for plenty of years

I've shed blood, sweat and tears

Friends came and went, family did too

I became stronger from the things I been through

I enjoyed the good times and survived the bad

Even when life made me so mad

I laughed, I cried, I smiled, I frowned

But I always kept my head up when I was down

Through the constant setbacks I kept on growing

I never stopped, I kept on going

My life has been a rollercoaster

But I'm going to ride it out until it's over

When My Time Comes

I have the feeling that my time is soon to come

My intuition tells me my days are almost done

Yet I have come to peace

With the thought of being deceased

I will not die in stress

After all, I have been blessed

The present as I know it will be my past

I will spend my future with God at last

Don't cry for me

I hope that you'll know

That it was my time

My time to go

Letter to My Child

To my dear child

If you read this after I go

This is your father

And I want you to know

That you are not alone

God is always with you

And I will always be with you too

I'm letting you know now

The roads will be rough

But those same roads

Will make you tough

Put God first and you will succeed

He will grant you everything that you need

There's nothing wrong with wanting to live nice

But remember everything comes with a price

Be careful of how you evaluate family and friends

Not everyone will be with you until the end

Things won't always go

According to planned

But never take life for granted

Enjoy it as much as you can

Because one day it will all be over

But until then

I'll live vicariously through you

Until we see each other again

Finally, Eternity

My flesh has expired

But my soul isn't done

Though my physical being has come to an end

The true me has just begun

Derrick had his reign

But he may no longer be

I will finally proceed to experience

My full potential as Eternity

Made in the USA
Columbia, SC
18 June 2021